Nottingham (

A Brief Histor

THERE has been a castle on this site for nearly a thousand years. As times have changed so has the Castle. Started by William the Conqueror, in 1068, it grew to become one of the most important Royal Castles in England. It was first and foremost an important fortification in the centre of England, on the River Trent, and the principal road to the North. From here the King could quickly move to conduct campaigns against both the Scots and the Welsh. As a result, it became a royal residence, and was lavishly maintained and embellished. It also served as an arsenal, a supply point, and a prison. The importance of the site is exemplified by the fact that it was here that both Richard III, and later Charles I, chose to raise their Standards and summon the people to arms.

The defeat and execution of Charles I in 1649, heralded the end of an era, and of the Castle. The local population were only too happy to see its destruction in 1651, since its very presence had put the Town in considerable danger during the Civil War. So with picks and shovels, and gunpowder, the great Castle came down; no longer did the walls of its great shell keep, with its high towers rising out of the very rock itself, dominate the skyline. What was left was substantially swept away by the Duke of Newcastle, who built his new Renaissance style Palace upon this great outcrop of rock. The building, whilst expressing the peace of the new age, still maintained the domination of

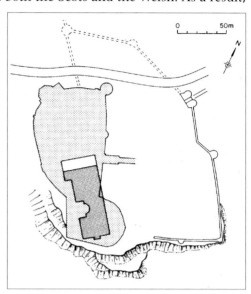

Relationship of the Medieval Castle to the Ducal Palace.

its inhabitant over the Town; the Dukes being men of considerable influence and power at Court, and Lord Lieutenants of the County.

This was to have serious repercussions in 1831, when the townspeople heard the news of the rejection of the Reform Bill by the House of Lords. After two days of disorder, the cry went up "To the Castle". The building was set alight. Thereafter it remained a gutted shell for more than 40 years. In 1878 it was restored by the Council as the first provincial Museum of Fine Art. In so doing, the Town, according to a contemporary account, "wiped out the stain which the lawless act of a former generation had cast upon them".

Daniel King's view of Nottingham Castle in 1660 (NCM).

It was not until 1908 that the Council acquired the allotment gardens that still occupied most of the Outer Bailey. They then set about restoring and repairing the Outer Bailey walls, with little or no consideration for their antiquity. It was believed that nothing remained of the former Castle and everything was done to turn the grounds into a municipal park. In fact, given its proximity to the centre of the Town, it is amazing just how much of the Castle has survived. This is undoubtedly due to the Dukes of Newcastle, who by converting the site into a ducal residence, ensured its preservation. It is now scheduled by the Department of the Environment as a Scheduled Ancient Monument.

A tapestry map of 1635 showing the Royal Castle and the churches of St Nicholas, St Marys and St Peters.

The Excavations

In 1976 the Nottingham Civic Society decided to finance a series of excavations at the Castle, which continued, on and off, for a period of ten years at a cost of over £100,000. The results of the excavations and historical research were subsequently published jointly by the Civic Society and Thoroton Society- "Nottingham Castle - A PLACE FULL ROYAL". Nature has also played its part in exposing the original Royal Castle, when on Christmas Day 1997, a burst water main caused part of the Duke's retaining wall to slip off the castle rock. It revealed the base part of the walls of the south west corner of the Upper Bailey, which had not been seen for three hundred years. Subsequently other parts of the Castle have been uncovered during building works. Excavations were also undertaken on the northern part of the Outer Bailey, before the redevelopment of Standard Hill.

There are only two surviving "plans" of the Castle. The first dated 1610 is a sketch by John Speede, inset into a plan of the Town. The second is a detailed plan of the Upper Bailey (Upper Court) and Middle Bailey (Castle Yard) drawn seven years later by John Smythson. This may have been commissioned by the Duke of Rutland, who probably intended to convert the Castle into a suitable residence.

The excavations have confirmed the accuracy of Smythson's plan of 1617. Because this was a Royal Castle the building works were recorded in the Royal Records. Historical research has now enabled us to identify many of the individual buildings and when they were built. To understand Smythson's plan it should be compared with the drawing on page 15 and the plans on the inside rear cover. The highest part of the Castle, on the left – southern side – is the Upper Court. This is in the form of a shell keep. High walls and towers surround the enclosed courtyard. Against the walls are two or three storied buildings, which include Henry III's Royal Apartments. In the yard is a circular flight of steps, the original entrance to Mortimer's Hole, which can still be seen.

Entry to the Upper Court was by way of a ramped stairway which lead over the Inner Moat. This ditch was built over at various times. One of the rock cut rooms which was entered from it (King

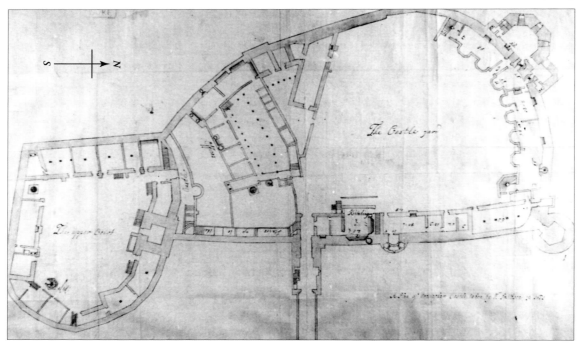

Smythson's Plan, 1617.

David's Dungeon), still survives (see page 9). It contains two pointed archways. These were probably built in about 1250, when a further building was constructed in the moat. Edward III was responsible for the last phase of building here. What is shown on the plan are most likely stables with offices and stores above. Access to the Upper Court could also be gained by stairs in the west wall; a flight still survives leading from the cave adjoining King David's Dungeon. (See page 8).

To the right of the plan is the Castle Yard. On the west wall (at the top of the plan) Romylow's Tower, and nearby, the Common Chapel. Against the east wall are a range of buildings running from the Middle Gate to the North-East Corner Tower (Black Tower). These include the Great Kitchen and the Constables Hall. Running along the north wall were the new State Apartments of Edward IV and behind them, the hexagonal Richard's Tower. The absence from the plan of the Great Hall, which stood in the middle of the Yard, confirms that by then it had fallen down. Both of these Baileys were protected by a second ditch, the Middle Moat, crossed by a draw bridge. Part of that bridge survives, as does the southern part of the Moat.

The walls of the Outer Bailey are not shown on Smythson's plan, but they are clearly visible on John Speede's sketch of 1610. This is aligned north/south and can be compared to the drawing on page 15 and Badder and Peats plan on page 18. The Gatehouse is shown, with one tower to the north, and the two surviving towers to the south. The accuracy of the sketch is more questionable in relation to the other baileys. In the Middle Bailey can be seen representations of the Middle Gate, the Black Tower, Royal Apartments(?), Richard's Tower, Chapel, and Romylow's Tower. What is the line across the yard? Is it a wall or a path – we simply do not know. The Upper Bailey is devoid of buildings. Perhaps Speede failed to gain access.

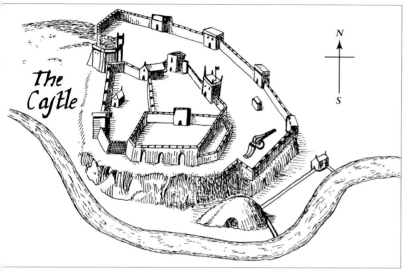

Part of Speede's Map, 1610.

The Outer Bailey was protected by a third ditch, the Outer Moat, and by the Gatehouse, which still survives to first floor level. It is one of only three surviving examples of the many built by Henry III. It was protected by gates, portcullis and a drawbridge, the latter being replaced by the existing stone bridge in the 1500s. The walls to the north of the Gatehouse disappeared after 1809. The land was then sold, and a new road constructed through the Castle to provide access to the Park, which the 4th Duke was then developing. Originally this wall connected to the Town Wall. In 1272 Henry III ordered the Burgesses of the Town to build a postern gate sufficient for "two armed horsemen with lances on their shoulders to pass through;" (Postern Street).

The Royal Castle
The Norman Fortress
(1068 - 1216)

Castles were unknown in England before the Norman Conquest in 1066, the Saxons defending their settlements with wooden palisades and ditches. The Normans were interested not in protecting the local population from attack, but in dominating and subjugating them. The standard Norman Castle was a "motte and bailey". At Nottingham, the motte, a high mound usually constructed from the earth dug out of the deep surrounding ditch, was constructed on the highest part of the rock. On it would be wooden buildings and perhaps a wooden watch tower, or keep. Below the motte, to the north, was the bailey similarly enclosed by a wooden palisade on an earth rampart. **William the Conqueror** (1066-87) built thirty such castles within five years of the Battle of Hastings; one of these was Nottingham Castle.

In 1068 William passed through Nottingham on his way to suppress a Saxon revolt in York. He would have seen the deserted Castle Rock rising up over 130 feet above the meadows of the River Trent. The location for a castle was ideal for two reasons. First, because the rock provided an easily defensible site dominating the country around, including the Saxon town huddled around St. Mary's Church, in what is now the Lace Market. Second, Nottingham was on the main road between London and the North, and was only a mile from the River Trent, the dividing line between the North and South of England, so it could be easily supplied and reinforced. The location, combined with impregnable defences, was to ensure that Nottingham Castle remained the principal Royal Fortress in the Midlands for five centuries.

Having decided upon this location, William ordered the building of a castle. The local population would have been forced to build their conqueror's castle, in whatever materials were available. The rock provided a natural motte or mound, and the original walls enclosing the baileys or yards, though probably being of wood, may have been supplemented by stone dug out of the surrounding ditch. Subjugation of the local population was completed by the building of a new Norman Town in the shadow of the Castle, with its own market place - the present Market Square. Land was also taken to the west of the Castle to make a park, which would be stocked with deer to provide food and sport, whilst to the south, the King's Meadow would be used for grazing.

Because the motte was natural rock, it would not be necessary to wait for the ground to settle before building high stone walls and towers on its summit. If these walls were not originally built of stone, they would have been by the reign of **Henry 1** (1100-35). These great stone walls with towers rising, as it were, from the very rock itself, and visible for miles in every direction, must have awed the local population. Below it, to the north, were the palisade walls of the Middle Bailey (now the Castle Green), and beyond them, to the north and east, more land was enclosed to form the Outer Bailey.

After Henry I's death in 1135, Civil War raged in England between the Empress Matilda and King **Stephen** (1135-54). The Castle was held for Stephen by the Constable, William Peveril. In 1140 the Earl of Gloucester burnt the town, but failed to capture the Castle. The following year Stephen's army was defeated at Lincoln. Peveril was forced to give up the Castle, but not for long. In 1142 he recaptured it with a small band of soldiers. They scaled the Castle Rock, guided by two young men who tended the Castle mill, and "took the citadel and hurled out of the Town" supporters of the Empress.

The Castle c.1200. The Outer Bailey is defended by a ditch and wooden palisade, whilst other parts are now enclosed by stone walls with two substantial stone towers. The Royal Apartments are in the Upper Bailey. The Great Hall and other domestic buildings are in the Middle Bailey.

In 1153 the Town was again burnt, this time by Matilda's son, the Duke of Normandy, later **Henry II** (1154-89). He did not attempt to capture the Castle, realising, according to a contemporary account, "that it could not be taken by storm, or, well supplied as it was, starved into submission, the site being by nature impregnable, he abandoned the futile task". The following year Henry became King. He arrived in Nottingham in 1155 and took possession of the Castle. Peveril, reputedly disguised as a monk, fled, first to his monastery at Lenton and then abroad.

Henry carried out extensive improvements to the Castle, for henceforth it was, together with Winchester and Windsor, to be a Royal Palace as well as a fortress. In 1171 the defences were greatly improved by the replacing of the wooden palisade enclosing the Middle Bailey with a high stone wall. (Parts of these walls are visible beside the driveway- excavated in 1986/7). It had a great square tower over the gateway and a new stone drawbridge over the middle moat. The living accommodation in the Upper Bailey was improved by the construction of several new buildings, including the "King's bed chamber" and the "King's chamber". In 1180 Henry ordered the building of a great hall in the centre of the Middle Bailey at a cost of £250. It was a substantial building with aisles, like a great church, large enough for meetings of the King's Council of Barons, for the holding of Parliaments, and for entertainment.

Henry also built a "house for the King's falcons" at the Castle, and repaired the royal hunting lodge at Clipstone in Sherwood Forest. He was, according to a contemporary account, "addicted to

The remains of the Middle Bailey wall built by Henry II, excavated in 1976, with Tower of St Marys Church in far distance.

hunting beyond measure, at crack of dawn he was off on horseback, traversing wastelands, penetrating forests and climbing the mountain tops."

Richard I "The Lion-Heart" (1189-99) only visited England twice during his reign, spending the majority of his time in France or on the Third Crusade. Before he left England, he granted the former Peveril estates, excluding Nottingham Castle, to his brother Prince John. However, in 1191 John seized the Castle. Richard, on his return from the Crusade in 1194, found this, and several other castles, held by John's supporters. All but Nottingham surrendered.

On 25 March 1194 Richard arrived in Nottingham "with such a vast multitude of men, and such a clangor of trumpets and clarions, that those who were in the Castle were astonished and confounded and alarmed, and trembling came upon them". The defenders, however, would not accept that the King had come and, thinking that it was a plot, they refused to surrender. So Richard, in plain armour, and preceded by a bodyguard carrying large shields, led the assault. A bloody battle ensued, the King himself killing a defender in close combat, with an arrow. By nightfall the wooden gateway to the Outer Bailey had been captured and burnt, but the defenders lay secure behind King Henry's high stone walls of the Middle Bailey.

The next day the King ordered stone throwing engines to be brought from his siege train to Nottingham. He then hanged, in full view of the defenders, some men at arms captured the previous day. Realising that a further assault would be costly, he summoned the Archbishop of Canterbury to Nottingham to excommunicate the defenders in the hope that they would surrender. On the following day the Bishop of Durham brought additional forces, but it was not until the arrival of the Archbishop of Canterbury, on the 28th, that the defenders were eventually persuaded to surrender. The King then entered the Castle. He spared the garrison, accepting ransoms, and ordering the sale of the captured stores, which realised over £145. Three days later he held a Council in the Great Hall, when he banished his brother from England, a decision he was later persuaded to reverse.

The Robin Hood statue, near the site where Richard probably stood when attacking the Castle.

Richard left Nottingham soon after. Little work seems to have been done to improve the defences during the remainder of his reign. However, a "postern giving access to the motte" (Upper Bailey) was under construction between 1194-95. This may well be the 100 yard long passage cut through the castle rock, now known as Mortimer's Hole, which gives access to the Upper Bailey from the brewhouse and mills in the yard below.

John (1199-1216) visited the Castle two or three times a year, enjoying both the security of its walls and the entertainment of hunting, in both the Royal Park, below the Castle, and in Sherwood Forest. The defences of the Castle were strengthened by the building of a new stone tower in the Upper Bailey and by the refortification and extension of the Outer Bailey. There may also, at this time, have been a fourth bailey, the Northern Bailey. This Bailey was probably never fully enclosed and appears to have fallen into disuse by the 14th Century. The household accounts show, amongst other payments, "the sum of 7d. to William the waterbearer for baths taken by the King". But life was not all entertainment, and as befitted his troubled reign he used the Castle, as many of his successors were later to do, as a military arsenal (which included the making of catapults), a treasury and a prison. Twenty-eight Welsh hostages were held here in 1212. John, hearing of the treachery of their fathers, hurried to Nottingham and ordered them to be hanged from the battlements.

The Plantagenet Palace (1216 - 1437)

Henry III (1216-72), spent considerable sums of money transforming the Castle, both improving its defences and making it a suitable residence for himself and his Queen. Provision had to be made during the King's frequent visits, for the Royal Family, men at arms, barons, clerks and servants, numbering up to 100 persons. Accommodation had to be provided for them and their horses, and the vast quantities of food they would require during their stay, which might be as long as a fortnight.

The royal records reveal substantial expenditure, not only on repairs and rebuilding, but on "beautifying" the apartments. Many chambers were plastered, some were painted with classical or biblical scenes, the windows glazed, often with stained glass, the walls wainscotted (panelled) and the rooms lit by iron candelabra. Some impression of the size and importance of the Castle can be gathered from the fact that there were then three Halls; the Great Hall, the King's Hall and the Queen's Hall, and six Chapels; three of them, the King's Chapel, the Chapel of St. Nicholas and "the small Chapel of the Queen's Chamber", were in the Upper Bailey. Of the remaining three, the Great Chapel was in the Middle Bailey, the Chapel of St. Mary of the Rock was in the Park, and the Chapel of St. James "outside the Castle" was in St. James's Street.

The defences of the Castle were further strengthened, between 1252-55, by the replacement of the palisade around the Outer Bailey with a stone curtain wall. Henry, having spent Christmas at the Castle in 1251, ordered the Sheriff to carry out this work, and to build "a good stone gateway with twin towers (the Gatehouse) and two round towers with loopholes at the angles of the yard open towards the Castle". The enclosure of the Outer Bailey by this wall completed the stone defences of the Castle which, thus fortified had, in the words of the thirteenth century chronicler Wykes "no peer in the Kingdom of England".

On succeeding his father, **Edward I** (1272-1307) did not return to England from Sicily for two years. During this period the country was governed by a three-man Council, one of whom, Archbishop Gifford, was Constable of the Castle. To prevent the possibility of disorder, he banned a tournament at the Castle in 1272, ordering the participants not to "make jousts, seek adventures, or in anyway go in arms."

Edward visited the Castle in 1279, 1280 and 1290. Although it did not feature directly in his campaigns against the Scots and Welsh, many prisoners were kept there. Edward spent £1,017, a considerable sum, on keeping the Castle in

The Castle c.1300. The Gatehouse and Outer Bailey Walls add to the defences of the Castle as do the addition of towers in the other Baileys including the Black Tower. To the north (right) is the Northern Bailey enclosed by a wooden palisade.

repair and improving its defences. The works would have included the strengthening of the stone walls and the building of several towers, including the semi-circular tower and Black Tower in the Middle Bailey, and the addition of a large round tower near the Gatehouse to the Outer Bailey - Edward's Tower.

The Castle was well provisioned and the King ordered the Constable "to keep the Castle so well provided and safely kept that damage or danger shall not arise in any way to the King or the Castle for lack of munition or custody".

The gains made by Edward against the Scots were soon lost by his son **Edward II** (1307-27). He was ultimately unable either to subdue the Scots, who under Robert the Bruce had raided deep into Yorkshire, or to secure his hold on his own Crown. This breakdown of law and order is exemplified by the murder of the Mayor of Nottingham in 1313, and the subsequent attack on the

A dramatic view of the capture of Mortimer from a print of 1836.

Castle by the Burgesses of the Town. In 1315 they besieged the Castle for eight days. The garrison was probably very small, being probably only ten men-at-arms and twenty foot soldiers, as was usual unless the Castle was threatened by an attacking army.

The Castle was, nevertheless, kept in repair, "the King willing that his Castle should be defended for the greater security and tranquillity of his people". In 1312 a Peel, or enclosed yard, was constructed in the Park to hold provisions for the King's armies in the North. The Sheriff received that year alone, "for Nottingham Castle 50 quarters of wheat, 60 quarters of malt, 40 quarters of oats, two tuns of wine, 10 guarts of salt, 10 carcasses of beef, 30 bacon pigs, 500 of stock fish, 2 meise of herring and 20 cart loads of wood". This use of the Castle typifies its strategic location as a supply point far enough south to be safe from attack by the Scots. Edward frequently spent Christmas at the Castle, and his wife, Queen Isabella, sought refuge there in 1319, after the Scots had attempted to kidnap her at York.

The strength of Nottingham Castle, however, was not to prevent the King's overthrow in 1327, and his subsequent incarceration and murder at Berkeley Castle, by Roger Mortimer, Earl of March. The new King, **Edward III** (1327-77), was only 15. The Kingdom was now ruled by Mortimer and his mistress, Queen Isabella. In October 1330 they came to Nottingham to hold a Parliament. The young Edward with his wife and son, later the Black Prince, followed them to Nottingham. They lodged in the town, whilst Mortimer and his mistress remained secure in the Castle, protected by Welsh mercenaries. Edward, fearful that he might suffer the same fate as his father, entered into a plot to seize Mortimer and secure his birthright. At the dead of night on 19th October, the Constable, William de Eland, and 24 men arrived at a thicket in the Park. In the dark they failed to meet up with their fellow conspirators. Undaunted they proceeded with their task alone. They entered the Castle through a "postern in the Park", then, according to one account, they "mounted the stairs leading to the Upper Bailey and entered the Hall where the Queen was sitting in Council". As the conspirators burst in, two of the Queen's supporters cried out and tried to protect Mortimer. They were struck down, and Mortimer was overpowered as he tried to arm

"Edward's Tower", though much restored and lower than it would have been in the 14th century, still dominates the surrounding area.

himself and raise the alarm. By morning, Mortimer was on his way to London to be tried and executed, and the Castle was secured for the King.

During the next forty years, Edward undertook substantial new works at the Castle. The royal records reveal details of substantial repairs and new buildings in all parts of the Castle. In the Upper Bailey, the "little chamber" and granaries were pulled down and rebuilt, a new gateway with a tower was constructed, the bridge repaired, and many buildings re-roofed including the "King's Chapel". In 1348 this building had six new windows inserted by a London glazier with 25,228 lbs. of glass.

In 1368 the Constable, then Stephen Romylow, was ordered to build a new kitchen in the Middle Bailey, and to rebuild the Middle Gate and to construct a chamber at the Gate "complete with doors, windows, chimneys, garderobes and with two supporting arches, whereof one leads to the King's (Great) Hall and the other to the Upper Bailey". Romylow also built a 180 feet long wall connecting this Gate on the east with a new tower that he built on the western side of the Middle Bailey - Romylow's Tower. This wall enclosed all the domestic buildings in the Middle Bailey, which now included a new Constable's Chamber and Chapel. This had been completed in 1367, when it was whitewashed, paved and provided with a font, a bell and two chests for vestments and ornaments.

The steps, within the Middle Bailey Walls, leading down to King David's Dungeon.

The Gatehouse of the Outer Bailey was also repaired, as were "a great house" and other "houses", for the use by the itinerant Justices. All in all the Castle was greatly improved for the King and his Court. Edward held three Parliaments at the Castle, and one of them, in 1337, banned the wearing of foreign cloth except by members of the Royal Family, so protecting English cloth workers and laying down the foundations of England's greatness as a manufacturing country.

This Royal Palace was also a prison. Edward had ordered the building of a new prison beneath the Upper Bailey for the "Scottish prisoners". One of those prisoners may have included King David II of Scotland. He passed through Nottingham in 1346 on his way to the Tower of London. Legend has it that he languished here for eleven years in a rock cut dungeon, passing the time by carving the story of Christ on the rock walls with his fingernails! Others imprisoned here included the speaker of the House of Commons in 1374, and in 1392, **Richard II** (1377-99) imprisoned the Mayor, Aldermen and Sheriffs of the City of London.

Both Richard, and later **Henry IV** (1399-1413), who overthrew him in 1399, made frequent visits to the Castle. Richard usually visited in the summer months, holding both a Great Council here in 1388, and a Parliament in 1399. Henry granted the Castle to his wife, Queen Joan, in 1403 and she held it until her death in 1437. Over these two reigns, relatively large sums were spent on the Castle, principally on maintenance. The only substantial works undertaken being the rebuilding of three of the four mills in Brewhouse Yard, then named Sparrow, Donne, Dosse and Gloff.

"King David's Dungeon" – a cave room probably carved out of the rock in the 12th century, with two pointed arches that give access to undercrofts built during the reign of King John.

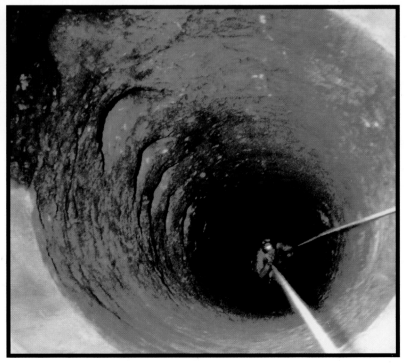

(Above): The north corner of Richard's Tower, excavated in 1978. To the right is the entrance to the spiral stairwell that led to the Royal Apartments above. To the left is a pit dug by Roundheads in 1651 to assist in the almost total demolition of the Tower.

(Above right): Richard's Tower - the south corner of the Tower before it was excavated, with the 100 foot well which had been used as a rubbish pit before it was cleared (right). In it was discovered a 16th century cannon.
(See page 14)

(Right): The Ducal Palace, on the site of the Upper Bailey dominates Brewhouse Yard - the location of the Castle brewhouse and mills, which could be reached by the 100 yard passage through the rock - Mortimer's Hole - the entrance of which can be seen in the centre of the picture. To the right is the Trip to Jerusalem, which claims to be the oldest Inn in England.

(Below): Mortimer's Hole. This passage, probably constructed in the 12th Century was originally protected by four gates. It provided a convenient short cut for bringing in supplies and a sally-port, so that the defenders of the Castle could surprise a besieging army.

(Above right and bottom): The Outer Bailey walls, restored - 1908, still give dramatic views over the Trent Valley. Much of the corner tower of 1252 survives.

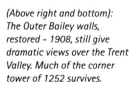

(Left): The Ducal Palace set ablaze by the mob on the night of 10th October 1831. The whole population turned out to watch the spectacular conflagration, many buying pieces of the Duke's tapestries as souvenirs.
(From a contemporary print by Thomas Allom).

(Left): Today in more tranquil times, with the canal in the foreground. Note the enormous flagpole which dominated the restored building for over 100 years before its removal in June 1999.

Visitors to the Ducal Palace would ascend the Grand stairway to the Eastern Terrace (below right). From there they climbed further steps (now demolished) to the main entrance on the first floor (above), beneath the impressive statue of the First Duke on horseback, sadly mutilated by rioters in 1831 (below). The whole building is perched dramatically on the very edge of the rock, part of which fell away in 1997.

The Wars of the Roses
(1437 - 1485)

Neither **Henry V**, nor his son **Henry VI**, showed any particular interest in the Castle. It was not until the reign of **Edward IV** (1461-83), and the internal upheavals of the Wars of the Roses, that the strategic position of Nottingham again became important. Edward proclaimed himself King at Nottingham in 1461. He appointed his brother, the Duke of Gloucester, later Richard III, to command his armies in the North.

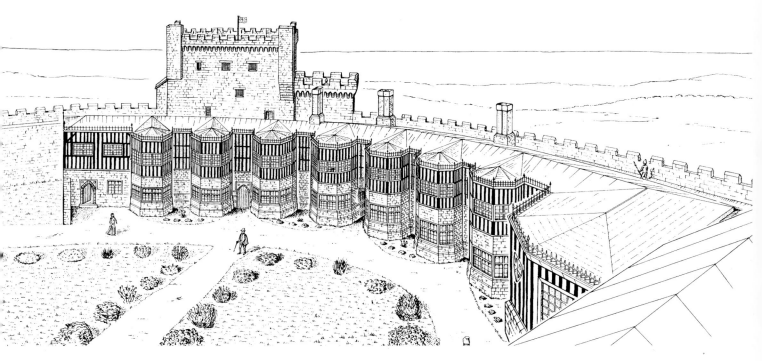

A reconstruction of the State Apartments with Richards Tower behind.

Between 1476 and 1480 Edward spent over £3000 in creating a new Royal Palace at the Castle. Richard would have supervised the erection of this last and greatest series of buildings on the northern wall of the Middle Bailey. These new State Apartments, with a curved range of seven bay windows, elaborately framed in timber on the first floor, overlooked the Middle Bailey Courtyard. They were built entirely for comfort, rather than defence, which was provided by a new enormous six sided tower, Richard's Tower. Built behind the new apartments, rising to a height of probably sixty feet, this tower was almost a castle in its own right. It must have been the most impressive feature of the Castle's fortification. Fifty years later, a visitor described these new buildings as "the bewtifullest part and gallant building for Lodgyng... a right sumptuus pece of stone work".

Probably for this reason, **Richard III** (1483-85) used the Castle during his short and turbulent reign as his principal residence and military base. It was here that he received the news of his son's death, thereafter referring to it as his "castle of care." It was here, too, that he heard of Henry Tudor's invasion. When, on the 19th of August 1485, he raised his Standard and left the security of its walls to lose his life and crown at the Battle of Bosworth, this great fortress could indeed be described by Skelton as "a place full royall".

Dekay and Ruyne
(1485 - 1642)

The death of Richard III saw the end of both the Wars of the Roses, and of an era, for Nottingham Castle. Although it was to remain, for the next hundred years, the principal Royal Fortress in the North Midlands, the introduction of both artillery and of stable central Government in London were combining to make castles obsolete.

A reconstruction of how the Cannon might have looked when it was built in about 1500.

Henry VII (1485-1509) visited the Castle in 1486, 87 and 89. The records reveal that the only work that was carried out was repairing the lead roofs. However, during the reign of his son, **Henry VIII** (1509-47), a survey of "the dekay and ruyne of the said castell" in 1525, reported among other things, that: "Part of the roof of the Great Hall is fallen down. Also the new building there (the State Apartments) is in dekay of timber, lead and glass" as, apparently, were many other parts of the Castle, including "the King's Chapel" and "the Lord Steward's lodging over the buttery". However, "dekay and ruyne" probably means no more than in need of repair, for money was still being spent on the Castle. Henry ordered new tapestries, presumably for the State Apartments, before his only visit in August 1511. It was to be the last time a reigning monarch would actually stay at the Castle. An inventory on his death in 1547 reveals that there were still forty-five tapestries in the Castle.

The Cannon found in King Richard's Tower in 1978.

In 1536 the Castle was "fortified and victualled" and was "layed roundabout with gunnys". The garrison, which probably by then amounted to less than a dozen men, was increased to four or five hundred. Such a dramatic increase in power was required to quell the Pilgrimage of Grace, a rebellion against the King's religious policies, which had spread from Yorkshire to Lincolnshire. With the suppression of this uprising, the garrison was stood down and the substantial armoury dispersed. Such hectic activity was not again to be seen at the Castle for a hundred years.

The upkeep of the fabric of the Castle was, however, causing a constant drain on the Exchequer; many of the walls and buildings being already over 400 years old. In 1538, the Earl of Rutland, who was then Constable, stressed, not for the last time, the need for repairs, pointing out that "40s. spent now, will save £40 in the future". Some money was made available, and the Earl may have been responsible for rebuilding the Middle Bridge, and for its decoration with statues of beasts and giants. The repairs that were undertaken to relieve the ravages of time were obviously not adequate. During the reign of **Queen Elizabeth I** (1558-1603), he wrote again, in 1560, to her Treasurer "concerning the dekay of the quene's castell of Nottingham and the needful repair the same doth require". He was told, in typical Civil Service fashion, that money would be forthcoming from "tyme to tyme... and then I trust you shall have the castell brought to good repair, except those things wherein utter ruyne ys in."

The Castle was visited in 1540 by the historian Leland, who gives us, for the first, time an account of a walk around the building: "The Outer Bailey is large and mighty strong, and there is a stately bridge (with pillars bearing beasts and giants) over the ditch into the Middle Bailey, the front of which at the entrance is exceeding strong, with towers and portcullises. Within is a fair green court fit for any princely exercise. The south-east parts of the Castle are strong and well-towered; within the old tower there is another court the Upper Bailey though somewhat less than the last mentioned, in the midst whereof there is a staircase of stone about six or seven feet above ground, in which there is a door to enter and steps to lead through the main rock to the foot thereof and the bank of the River Leen (Mortimer's Hole)."

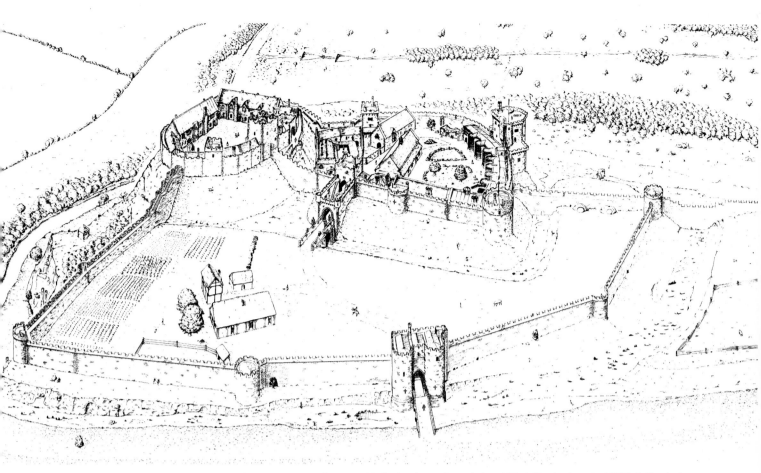

The Castle as it may have looked in 1485. In the foreground is the Gatehouse. Beyond, the middle bridge leads to the Middle Bailey. In the centre of which is the Great Hall and behind it, the Chapel and Romylow's Tower. To the right are the new State Apartments and Richard's Tower. To the left is the ramped stairway leading to the Upper Bailey, the entrance of which is protected by the High Tower.

Some further repairs were completed for the proposed visits of Queen Elizabeth in 1562 and 1574. On the first occasion she was to have met Mary, Queen of Scots, but the meeting, and both visits to Nottingham, were abandoned. Further repairs were carried out, the last being in 1605 when £5 was spent, but the Castle was never again to provide a residence for royalty. It did, however, provide a medieval backdrop in 1612, when the local gentry were presented to **James I** (1603-25). During their visits to Nottingham, both he, and later his son, **Charles I** (1625-49), preferred the comforts of Thurland Hall (which stood on Pelham Street), the residence of the Earls of Clare.

A Victorian view of the Castle in 1617 as it might have appeared, from T.C. Hine's History of the Castle.

In 1617 Smythson drew the only surviving plan of the Royal Castle. It may have been drawn for the Earl of Rutland, the hereditary Constable of the Castle. He may have envisaged turning it into a stately home, as one of his successors was to do at Belvoir Castle. If that was the original intention, it was not pursued, for when the now dilapidated Castle was sold to the Earl by James I in 1623, he seems to have actively encouraged its further decay. The Great Hall had by then fallen down, and the Earl himself proceeded to despoil the Castle of "tymbre, lede and tyle".

The Civil war (1642 - 1660)

Charles I raising his standard from a contemporary engraving.

Whatever the state of the fabric in 1642, the Castle still dominated the skyline, towering over the Town beneath it. Just as Richard III had chosen it as his rallying point in 1485, so now Charles I came here to raise his Standard and summon an army to his side. The Standard was first raised on 22nd August on Derry Mount, just outside the Outer Bailey, and was carried in to the Castle at night. This was to mark the declaration of war between King and Parliament, which was to end in the King's surrender five years later, at Newark.

The war started badly for the King. The response to his call to arms was poor, and realising that the Town's sympathies largely lay with Parliament, he left Nottingham. This allowed the Parliamentarians to seize the Castle, and Colonel John Hutchinson, a local landowner, and later to be one of the signatories of the King's death warrant, was appointed its Governor. His wife, Lucy, recorded that she found it "very ruinous and uninhabitable, neither affording room to lodge soldiers nor provisions". In her diary she described Mortimer's Hole and continued: "In the midway… there is a little piece of the rock on which a dovecote had been built, but the Governor took down the roof of it and made it a platform for two or three pieces of ordinance which commanded some streets and all the meadows better than the Upper Bailey". In the Middle Bailey "there had been several towers and many noble rooms, but most of them were down", and beyond the Middle Gate "there was a very large yard, the Outer Bailey, that had been walled, but the walls were all down… and there were the ruins of an old pair of gates with turrets on each side. In the whole rock there were many large caverns, where a great magazine and many hundred soldiers might have been disposed, and might have been kept secure from any danger of firing the magazines by any mortar pieces shot against the castle".

Colonel Hutchinson.

Considerable efforts were obviously made to make the Castle habitable for the garrison of four hundred men and to repair and adapt the defences for cannon. The defenders repulsed numerous attacks by the Royalists from Newark, but in January 1644 it looked as if all were lost. The Governor had built earthworks in the Meadows to protect Trent Bridge. He had, however, wisely refused to remove the guns from the Castle, for when, on the morning of 15th January, the Royalists attacked, the Round-heads abandoned their positions and fled to the Castle, along with the Mayor and everyone else in the Town.

The cannon in the Castle "played upon" the attacking Royalists, taking "off wholly the second file of Musketeers". The commander, Sir Charles Lucas, then placed his soldiers in the houses around the Castle so that they could fire into it. The

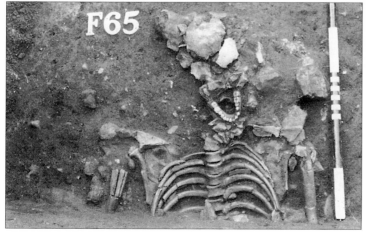

A Cival war casualty buried by the Chapel, which was then being used as a hospital. Excavated in 1978.

Governor, dismayed at the retreat of his forces, set about organising a counter attack, just as he had done the year before in August when much the same thing had happened. Then the Royalists had used the tower of St. Nicholas' to fire into the Castle, but that was no longer available to them since the Governor had wisely had the church pulled down.

Sir Charles Lucas wrote a letter threatening to sack and burn the town if the Castle were not surrendered. Being unable to find anyone to deliver his letter Sir Charles "took the mayor's wife, and with threats, compelled her to undertake it; but just as she went out of the house, she heard an outcry, that "the roundheads were sallying forth", and indeed they were. There followed vicious fighting in the streets leading to the Castle. The Royalists, numbed by the cold and exhausted by their march through the snow, eventually fled, leaving "a great track of blood, which froze as it fell upon the snow". The wounded were taken to the Chapel, which served as a hospital. One of the less fortunate may have been buried there. Part of his, or her, skeleton being excavated in 1978.

After the King's defeat peace returned to the town. In May 1651 the Parliamentary Council of State ordered the slighting of the Castle. Never taken by storm, it was finally demolished from within by gunpowder and the picks and shovels of the local population.

The Ducal Palace
As a Residence (1674 - 1831)

The work of the Parliamentary Government was to be completed, not by a Roundhead, but by the leader of the King's armies in the north. In 1663, after the restoration of Charles II (1660-85),

William Cavendish 1st Duke of Newcastle.

William Cavendish, who had been created the First Duke of Newcastle, purchased the Castle from the Duke of Buckingham. He proceeded to sweep away what remained above ground of the Upper Bailey, in order to build his Renaissance-style Palace, which still dominates the Castle Rock today. Only the caves survived, being turned into wine cellars. The Middle Bailey was lowered and grassed over to form a green, surrounded by a low wall. The "ruinated walls" of the Outer Bailey survived, and the Outer Gatehouse became a porters' lodge.

The building was completed in 1679, after the Duke's death, at a cost of £14,000. The entrance was on the east front, which was the most elaborately decorated side, with columns and scroll work. As befitted the custom, the principal rooms were on the first floor. They were entered via double flights of stairs, on both the east and west fronts, leading to a substantial Hall. The dining room lay at the north end of this Hall, and beyond that, at a lower level, were the kitchens. At the south end of the Hall were the drawing room and gallery. Below the gallery (where the restaurant now is) was an arcade, open to the south, where guests could stroll if the weather made the eastern terrace unsuitable.

Some of the splendour of the old Royal Castle, not seen for two hundred years, then briefly returned to Nottingham. The well-furbished palace provided a comfortable residence for Princess Anne, who stayed there before she became Queen in 1702, and for successive Dukes, one of whom, Thomas Pelham-Holles, was twice Prime Minister between 1755-1762. A visitor at this time described the rooms "of noble dimensions, furnished in half modern style, the drawing-room being adorned with velvet curtains and cabinets of Louis XIV." Some rooms had family portraits inserted in the wall panelling, others were hung with tapestries. The walls of the ballroom were covered with gilt impressed leather, which must have glistened like gold in the candle light.

The last Great Ball was held here in 1776. However, the industrialisation of the Town gradually diminished the attraction of this Ducal Palace as a residence. For the next fifty years it was used first as a boarding school, and later as apartments. The gardens were let off as allotments and those who had been used "to inhaling the breezes which swept the summit of the rock" were denied access by "his portership at the lodge who growls a denial… except his temper be sweetened with a bribe."

The Duke's Palace, though unoccupied, remained a symbol of his power. When news arrived in Nottingham, in October 1831, of the Duke's opposition to the Reform Bill, it was against this symbol that people turned. The Castle was to undergo its last siege and, with its defences down, it was to succumb. On the night of the 10th, a large crowd gathered outside the Gatehouse shouting abuse at the Duke and his building. They tried to force the wooden doors, which,

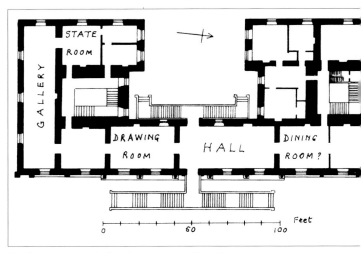

The State rooms on the first floor where royalty and distinguished guests were entertained and would sleep. The ground floor had a servants hall and similar minor rooms. The kitchens were at cellar level to the north.

to this day still protect the Castle at night. Unable to break through, they smashed the fencing at the side. The mob burst through and they rushed up the hill to the deserted Palace.

The Mayor and Constables could do nothing. The windows were smashed; the equestrian statue of the Duke, over the east door, was mutilated, and the contents of the building, such as they were, were looted. The citizens of France could not have done better, as the Palace was set ablaze. Molten lead poured off the building and fell burning to the ground as the mob looked on in amazement. This "outrage" caused considerable disquiet to the Government and undoubtedly, in its way, must have helped to ensure the passing of the Reform Bill in the following year.

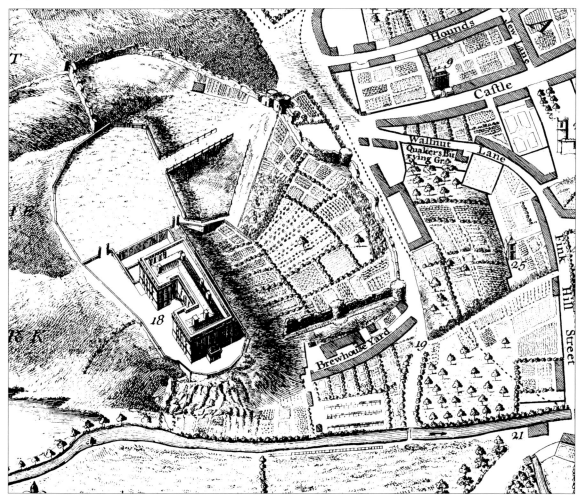

Part of Badder and Peats map of the town in 1744. By 1800 the area beyond the ruined walls of the Outer Bailey had become industrialised, factory chimneys belching out smoke over the Castle.

The Castle Museum
(1875 - Present day)

Despite receiving £21,000 in damages, the 5th Duke left the building as a blackened and gutted shell, looking down over the Town for forty years. Various suggestions were made to the Duke's successors as to what might be done with it. The 6th Duke, thankfully, rejected proposals to convert it into a prison or court, or to develop it with housing as part of The Park. The northern part of the Outer Bailey having already been built on after the construction of Lenton Road in 1808. He eventually agreed to it being converted into a museum, so ensuring the preservation of the site for future generations.

In 1875 the Council took a lease on the building, and T. C. Hine, a prominent local architect, began the restoration. Unfortunately, electricity being in its infancy, in order to get as much daylight as possible into the rooms, the three floors of the original Palace were replaced by only two. The entrance stairs on the eastern front had already been removed to allow the Robin Hood Rifles to drill more conveniently. Those on the western side were replaced by a colonnade. In order to provide access for vehicles, a new driveway was cut around the Castle Green, so destroying any trace of the royal apartments.

On July 3rd 1878, the Mayor and Corporation gathered at the Castle to see the opening of the first provincial Museum of Fine Art. The ceremony was performed by the Prince of Wales, later Edward VII. He entered the Castle through the Gatehouse, that so many of his predecessors had passed through before him.

Since then, the Museum has undergone many changes. The entrance is now on the ground floor, immediately beneath the Dukes' original entrance on the first floor. There are many interesting sections including Local History, the Sherwood Foresters as well as Art Galleries and Ceramic Exhibitions. Tours of Mortimer's Hole may be booked here.

THE GATEHOUSE SHOP

*The shop is run by the Nottingham Civic Society and manned entirely by volunteers.
It is full of information and souvenirs of Nottingham, sold to raise money for conservation work in the City.*

It is open from 11am to 4pm from Easter to October and thereafter at weekends.

Acknowledgements

I am grateful for the advice and assistance of Christopher Drage (T.V.A.R.C. – Nottingham University) who directed the excavations and allowed me to use his research into the Castle, Richard Sheppard for his drawings and maps of the Royal Castle and the cannon, Alan MacCormick, Ken Brand and the late Professor Maurice Barley for their invaluable help and encouragement, and Dr Foulds of the Castle Museum, and particularly to the late Thoresby Bradley, for running the Civic Society Shop at the Gatehouse for so many years, and to all the helpers who continue to give of their time to raise money for the Society.

Principle sources: C.J. Drage "A Place Full Royal", H.M. Colvin, "The History of the King's Works"

Design & Print by Parker and Collinson Limited, Church Street, Lenton, Nottingham NG7 2FH. July 1999

Tour of the Castle Grounds

(There are very helpful information panels in the grounds and a model in the Museum)

THE GATEHOUSE (1252-55) Built by Henry III, it is one of only three, of the many he built, to survive. It originally had another floor. It was protected by gates, secured by a wooden beam, portcullis and drawbridge over the Outer Moat. The Outer Bridge can best be seen from the Moat; the arch to the right being 13th Century and the other being a 16th Century replacement of the drawbridge. Once through the Gatehouse one enters the Outer Bailey.

THE BLACK TOWER - NORTH EAST CORNER TOWER (c.1270 - excavated 1976) The driveway, constructed in 1878, cuts through the eastern side of the Middle Bailey Wall. The Tower was probably 50 feet high when built. The lower section only survives, the remainder being destroyed after 1651.

THE MIDDLE BAILEY WALL (c.1170 - excavated 1976-8) Built by Henry II into the sand rampart constructed by William the Conqueror in 1068. It later formed the rear wall of the State Apartments built by Edward IV (c.1475). These Apartments and most of the wall were destroyed in 1651. Now only the foundation of the wall remains, on top of which the Duke of Newcastle constructed his boundary wall. Further up the driveway is a stairwell, which formerly led down to the base of King Richard's Tower (c.1476), re-excavated 1978/9.

THE MIDDLE BAILEY Beneath the grassed area of the Castle Green lie the remains of walls and towers excavated in 1980. In the centre once stood the Great Hall where many Parliaments were held. Near to the shrubs on the left of the driveway a skeleton was excavated in 1978, possibly indicating the site of the Great Chapel. (The play area was put here in 1998).

THE COURTYARD Formerly the Carriage House and stables of the Ducal Palace, which now covers the whole of the Upper Bailey and Inner Moat. Beneath you lies King David's Dungeon and the site of King John's bakehouse, excavated and refilled in 1981.

THE DUCAL PALACE (now the Castle Museum) Built in 1679 by the Duke of Newcastle. Originally, double flights of stairs on both the east and west sides led to the main doors to the hall on the first floor. These were removed some time after the building was gutted in 1831 during the Reform Riots. The colonnade on the west front dates from 1878, when the building was converted into a museum. The east front is decorated with Corinthian columns, rusticated stonework and elaborate window ornament. Above the centre window, formerly the eastern entrance, is a statue of the First Duke of Newcastle on horseback, mutilated in 1831.

MORTIMER'S HOLE Tours are available and recommended. The original entrance of this passage, which leads down to Brewhouse Yard, is still visible, though the tower that stood above it has gone. On the west side of the terrace can be seen the only surviving parts of the Upper Bailey walls, exposed in 1997 when part of the terrace fell off the rock. The Royal Apartments, chapels, guard house and granary that formerly stood in the Upper Bailey, surrounded by high walls and towers have disappeared forever. Note the view, including Wollaton Hall (1588), the University, the River Leen (now the Nottingham Canal), the Inland Revenue (built appropriately on what used to be the King's Meadow) and beyond, the River Trent.

THE DUKE'S STEPS Guests arriving at the Ducal Palace would alight from their carriage at the bottom of this grand flight of steps and ascend to the terrace above. The steps follow the line of the original steps that led from the Middle Bailey of the Royal Castle up to the Upper Bailey.

THE MIDDLE BRIDGE (c.1170) In the 16th century the drawbridge was removed and the rounded arch added. It was the only entrance to the Middle Bailey from the Outer Bailey and was protected by a Tower, part of which lies buried under the grass bank. It still crosses the line of the Middle Moat, which can be clearly seen to the right. The block of stones to the left came from the Town Wall; placed here in 1898.

THE OUTER BAILEY WALL (1252, restored 1908). Built by Henry III, the wall, then much higher, probably ran up the side of the cliff to the Upper Bailey above. Below can be seen Brewhouse Yard, the site of the Castle Mills and Brewhouse.

EDWARD'S TOWER (c.1300) This Tower was probably added by Edward I. A fine view can be obtained of the Outer Bridge and also over the town, including the Tower of St. Mary's (centre of the Saxon town), the Council House (centre of the medieval town), and the red brick tower of St. Nicholas' Church built in 1680. The original church was demolished in 1643, after it had been used by Royalists to fire on the Parliamentary forces holding the Castle.